An Introduction to Hacking and Crimeware

A Pocket Guide

An Introduction to Hacking and Crimeware

A Pocket Guide

VICTORIA LOEWENGART

IT Governance Publishing
IT Governance Limited
Unit 3, Clive Court
Bartholomew's Walk
Cambridgeshire Business Park
Ely
Cambridgeshire
CB7 4EH
United Kingdom

www.itgovernance.co.uk

First published in the United Kingdom in 2012
by IT Governance Publishing.

ISBN 978-1-84928-328-1

PREFACE

I hope you find this short pocket guide an educational and interesting read. This pocket guide is an introduction into the dark world of the business of cybercrime. It is not an in-depth analysis of malicious software code, but rather a foundation level overview to make you, the reader, aware of the existence of this world.

The information for this pocket guide came from many sources, including the Internet, "deep web" (i.e. subscription content), trade conferences, trade literature, and academic publications. I am also fortunate to have many friends who are information security professionals, and who were very kind in sharing their insights with me. This pocket guide is not just a compilation of information, but also a summary and analysis. I hope it whets your appetite enough to want to learn more about this subject.

Thank you!

Victoria

ABOUT THE AUTHOR

Victoria Loewengart has over 25 years' experience in all facets of "cyberspace" development, management, and exploration. She provided software solutions for business, federal government, research and development, and military organizations.

For most of her 25-year career Victoria worked in support of military and intelligence agencies and became fascinated with intelligence collection, analysis, cybersecurity, and counterintelligence techniques and technologies.

Currently Victoria is a partner/co-founder of AKOTA Technologies (*www.akotatech.com*) and Technology and Business Insider (TBI) (*www.insidertalk.net*).

Victoria is an Intelligence Studies scholar. She has conducted extensive research of the issues that affect intelligence and defense communities, including intelligence collection, cybersecurity, and competitive intelligence. Her articles have appeared in *BATTLESPACE TECHNOLOGIES* magazine (*www.battle-technology.com*).

Victoria is a bilingual Russian/English speaker. She conducts research in both languages with equal ease.

She has two brilliant college student daughters, and she lives in Columbus, OH, USA with her husband and her dog.

ACKNOWLEDGEMENTS

My undying love and gratitude to my husband Steve who makes all of my endeavors possible, to my parents who always believe in me, and to my daughters who keep me young and inspired.

Many thanks to my partners: Len Zuga at TBI (*www.insidertalk.net*) and Tom and Helena Keeley at AKOTA Technologies (*www.akotatech.com*) for keeping me interested and engaged.

Great thanks to Angela Wilde for expertly keeping together the process of getting this pocket guide ready for publication, and to Frances Insley for her excellent copy-editing work.

I would also like to express my gratitude to the reviewers; I was very encouraged by their remarks, and I appreciate the time they took to read my pocket guide and provide their comments: Jared Carstensen, Manager, Enterprise Risk Services, Deloitte & Touche; Chris Evans, IT Service Management Specialist, and Robin Smith MSc, Information and Intelligence Consultant.

Finally, thanks to IT Governance for giving me the opportunity to write this pocket guide.

CONTENTS

INTRODUCTION

"Cyberwarfare" ... "Cyberattacks" ... "Cyber espionage" – one cannot turn on a television set or open a newspaper without seeing these disturbing headlines. And indeed, the problem is serious. The news about "Stuxnet,"[1] "Night Dragon,"[2] and "Aurora"[3] attacks got the world worried about the vulnerability of global defense and industrial and financial infrastructures. The disruption of these systems could halt not just these institutions, but ultimately impede our entire networked civilization.

There is a perception that these attacks are carried out by sophisticated, often rogue, state-sponsored forces. While some of this perception is indeed based on reality, such as China's organized 9 to 5 hacking[4] or the sophisticated nature of the Stuxnet worm, many cyberattacks use relatively unsophisticated means. In fact, some of the toolkits to create viruses, botnets (defined later in this book), spyware, and other types of malware can be downloaded from the Web for free, or purchased for a low fee. The retailers of these tools function as legitimate businesses, and even provide 24/7 technical support for their products. This software can cause a lot of damage to civil and defense organizations alike.

---

[1] Stuxnet is a Windows® computer worm, discovered in July 2010, which targets industrial software and equipment. From: McAfee® Foundstone® Professional Services and McAfee Labs™. "Global Energy Cyberattacks: "Night Dragon"." McAfee. February 10, 2011. *www.mcafee.com/us/resources/white-papers/wp-global-energy-cyberattacks-night-dragon.pdf* (accessed April 23, 2011).

[2] Night Dragon is "coordinated covert and targeted cyberattacks [that] have been conducted against global oil, energy, and petrochemical companies." From *ibid.*

[3] Chinese hack-attack which started in mid-2009 and continued through December 2009, attacking Google™ networks. From *ibid.*

[4] Harris, Shane. "China's Cyber-Militia." National Journal. May 31, 2008. *http://nationaljournal.com/magazine/china-s-cyber-militia-20080531* (accessed April 20, 2011).

The emergence of the underground market of malware toolkits and malware applications made committing cybercrimes easier for the run-of-the-mill thieves and bank robbers who previously did not have the level of sophistication and the computer knowledge to do so. What are these toolkits? Where do they come from? Who makes them and who buys them?

The lines between cyberwarfare, cybercrime, cyber espionage, and cyberterrorism are blurred. Offensive cyber operations are defined as:

> operations to manipulate, disrupt, deny, degrade, or destroy information resident in computers and computer networks, or the computer net-work[*sic*] itself, or to gain control over the computer or computer network.[5]

With the availability of the commercial malware and malwarc toolkits, these activities are no longer limited to state-sponsored cyber forces, or even sophisticated technically savvy rogue hackers – anyone with intent and persistence can do it. Can commercially available malware become a secret weapon in cyberwarfare?

The purpose of this pocket guide is to bring to light the danger of commercially available malware tools and toolkits. In this pocket guide I will describe these malware toolkits and their producers and consumers. I will also explore commercial off-the-shelf (COTS) software tools that are not intended to be used as "hacking" tools, but could be used as such. I will discuss the implications of "malware for sale" in the context of a cyber conflict, and what it takes to fight back against this problem.

The information in this book is a result of extensive research that would not have been possible without the AKOTA document prioritization system from AKOTA Technologies (*www.akotatech.com*).

---

[5] HPCR Manual on International Law Applicable to Air and Missile Warfare. Program on Humanitarian Policy and Conflict Research, Harvard University. 2010. *www.ihlresearch.org/amw/manual/section-a-definitions/m* (accessed May 27, 2011).

CHAPTER 1: BACKGROUND

The software that is used to disrupt, steal, or manipulate is often referred to as malware, crimeware, or hackware. In this pocket guide these terms will be used interchangeably.

In recent years there has been an influx of commercially available "attack toolkits" to help wannabe hackers create and propagate their own malware without much technical knowledge of computer programming. The underground environment promotes entrepreneurship and allows buyers to subscribe to attack services or buy attack toolkits in bulk, using online shopping carts and paying via Western Union and PayPal.[6]

Attack toolkits are usually bundles of software libraries that can be used to put together an attack application. The pre-written code in these toolkits exploits new vulnerabilities found in commercial software (aka "Zero Day" vulnerabilities), as well as provides various tools to customize and automate attacks on networked computers, such as command-and-control (C&C) stealth server administration tools.[7] Attack kits are used to enable the theft of financial information and intellectual property information using bots,[8] as well as to convert compromised computers into a network of bots (aka botnet) in order to conduct additional attacks. These kits are advertised

---

[6] "Malware becoming increasingly commercialised, says CoreTrace." InfoSecurity. February 2, 2011. *www.infosecurity-magazine.com/view/15623/malware-becoming-increasingly-commercialised-says-coretrace/* (accessed May 10, 2011).

[7] "Report on Attack Toolkits and Malicious Websites." Symantec. *www.symantec.com/about/news/resources/press_kits/detail.jsp?pkid=attackkits&om_ext_cid=biz_socmed_twitter_facebook_marketwire_linkedin_2011Jan_worldwide_attacktoolkits* (accessed May 27, 2011).

[8] "A bot worm is a self-replicating malware program that resides in current memory (RAM), turns infected computers into zombies (or bots) and transmits itself to other computers." From: SearchSecurity. *http://searchsecurity.techtarget.com/definition/bot-worm* (accessed 30 November 2011).

and sold on online underground forums that trade stolen information and services.[9] The real strength of botnets lies in their ability to generate massive amounts of Internet traffic against specific targets. This is known as a distributed denial of service (DDoS) attack. Some well-known examples of DDoS attacks are Russian attacks against Estonia and Georgia, effectively shutting down all aspects of online life in these countries.[10] Of course, these attacks did not happen by themselves, but were allegedly initiated by Russian hacktivists.

Hacktivism is the act of hacking, or breaking into a computer system, for a politically or socially motivated purpose. The individual who performs an act of hacktivism is said to be a *hacktivist*.

A hacktivist uses the same tools and techniques as a hacker but does so in order to disrupt services and bring attention to a political or social cause.[11]

The danger of commercially available malware kits is that anyone can purchase them. What used to be the domain of the technically savvy is now open to anyone with an agenda to cause harm. Hacktivists can grow in numbers exponentially, because now they have the tools.

Creating malware, such as bots, is inexpensive and relatively easy. The business of buying and selling malware follows a well-established commercial model. Botnets are valued based on the structure of the botnet, past use/abuse of the botnet, location of the botnet's victims, and robustness of a malware

---

[9] "Report on Attack Toolkits and Malicious Websites." Symantec. *www.symantec.com/about/news/resources/press_kits/detail.jsp?pkid=attackkits&om_ext_cid=biz_socmed_twitter_facebook_marketwire_linkedin_2011Jan_worldwide_attacktoolkits* (accessed May 27, 2011) and "Malware becoming increasingly commercialised, says CoreTrace." *InfoSecurity*. February 2, 2011. *www.infosecurity-magazine.com/view/15623/malware-becoming-increasingly-commercialised-says-coretrace/* (accessed May 10, 2011).

[10] Carr, Jeffrey. *Inside Cyber Warfare: Mapping the Cyber Underworld*. O'Reilly Media, 2009. p.18.

[11] SearchSecurity. *http://searchsecurity.techtarget.com/definition/hacktivism)* (accessed May 27, 2011).

agent.[12] The sellers go as far as to guarantee damage, "or your money back."[13] YouTube even has tutorials on how to create the malware, deliver the bot agents, manage the C&C, and turn the stolen data into real money.[14]

Intentionally malicious software programs are not the only software that can be used for malicious purposes. Many mainstream, publicly available software applications can be utilized to steal or manipulate important data, and since everything these days is about cutting costs and implementing the least expensive solution, even military organizations can fall victim to clever use of the COTS software.

For example, in order to cut costs military satellite communications (SATCOM) adopted commercial satellites, and these assets are not protected from network and radio frequency (RF) attacks by adversaries using open-source and publicly available resources.[15] Both digital and analog signals can be captured, manipulated, and/or transmitted using open-source programs downloaded by hobbyists, or provided by equipment vendors and hacker websites complete with documentation and other resources.[16]

---

[12] Ollmann, Gunter. "How Criminals Build Botnets for Profit." Central Ohio InfoSec Summit, Columbus, OH. 2011.
[13] *Ibid.*
[14] *Ibid.*
[15] Rohret, David, and Jonathan Holston. "Exploitation of Blue Team SATCOM and MILSAT Assets for Red Team Covert Exploitation and Back-Channel Communications." *Proceedings of the International Conference on Information Warfare & Security.* 2010. 288–298. *International Security & Counter-Terrorism Reference Center*™, EBSCO*host*® (accessed May 14, 2011).
[16] *Ibid.*

CHAPTER 2: CRIMEWARE PRODUCTS

This chapter describes different varieties, and the evolution of, commercially available crimeware: from toolkits to exploit vulnerabilities of operating systems, to malware as a service, to crime accessories of cyber hooligans and thieves.

"Zero Day" exploit toolkits

In October of 2008, a commercial "Zero Day" attack pack was made available to the Chinese hacking community via a well-known public hacking repository website. The attack pack exploited a Microsoft® Windows® vulnerability, named MS08-067, which could allow remote code execution if an affected system received a specially crafted remote procedure call request.[17] As soon as this vulnerability became known, the MS08-067 port scanning toolkit with attack capability (the attack pack) went on sale, complete with user interface and the usage instructions.[18]

According to the researchers from major antivirus research labs, this kit allowed its "customers" to make money from pay-per-click sites using infected machines. This toolkit provided a DDoS attack option, could terminate popular antivirus software in China, and provided stealth capability.[19] The hacker even provided a customer service disclaimer that his tools must never be used for "legal purposes" and that they are sold for "research use" only. "For customer service [purposes], he has also warned his "customers" about "trojanized" versions of his

---

[17] "Microsoft Security Bulletin MS08-067 – Critical". Microsoft TechNet. October 23, 2008. *www.microsoft.com/technet/security/bulletin/ms08-067.mspx* (accessed May 23, 2011).

[18] Ren, Haowei. "Exploit-MS08-067 Bundled in Commercial Malware Kit." McAfee Labs. November 14, 2008. *http://blogs.mcafee.com/mcafee-labs/exploit-ms08-067-bundled-in-commercial-malware-kit* (accessed May 23, 2011).

[19] *Ibid.*

kit distributed by others on the Internet, that will install a backdoor to spy on the backdoor user."[20]

Toolkits like this are particularly dangerous, because they exploit systems' vulnerabilities that may be still unknown to the security community. Operating systems and browsers are the most targeted platforms for Zero Day attacks.

"Zeus"

Perhaps the most infamous commercial malware package is "Zeus", also known as "Zbot". Zeus is described as a malware package that is readily available for sale and also traded in underground forums. The package contains a builder that can generate a bot executable and web server files, such as images, PHP templates, and SQL templates, for use as the C&C server. Zeus is a generic back door that allows full control by an unauthorized remote user, and the primary function of Zeus is financial gain — stealing online credentials such as FTP, e-mail, online banking, and other online passwords.[21]

It has been alleged that Zeus was created by a Russian hacker with the code name "Slavik/monster". Since as early as 2008, Zeus has been readily available to buy in underground forums for as little as $700 and up to $8,000 for the newest version with all available features.[22] Ironically, the latest version of Zeus uses classic copy protection mechanisms to prevent the use of unlicensed pirate copies.[23]

---

[20] *Ibid.*

[21] Falliere, Nicolas, and Eric Chien. "Zeus: King of the Bots." Symantec Security Response. *www.symantec.com/content/en/us/enterprise/media/security_response/whitepapers/zeus_king_of_bots.pdf* (accessed May 23, 2011).

[22] *Ibid.*

[23] Stevens, Kevin, and Don Jackson. "ZeuS Banking Trojan Report." Dell SecureWorks. March 11, 2010. *www.secureworks.com/research/threats/zeus/?threat=zeus* (accessed May 19, 2010).

The biggest news story involving Zeus was about an international financial crime ring. The cyber thieves who used Zeus did not target large corporations or banks, but instead went after the accounts of medium-sized companies, towns, and even churches that did not have state-of-the-art security technology.[24] Using Zeus, hackers in Russia and Eastern Europe infected computers around the world.

The FBI found that the virus was carried in an e-mail, and when targeted individuals at businesses opened the e-mail, the malicious software installed itself on the victimized computers, secretly capturing passwords, account numbers, and other data related to financial accounts.[25]

Before being caught, the members of the theft ring managed to steal $70 million. In fact, this theft ring attempted to steal some $220 million and was actively involved in using Zeus to infect more computers.[26] They were caught thanks to the collaboration of international law enforcement organizations across international borders.[27]

Recently the source code for Zeus was released into the "wild," i.e. became available to anyone who wants it. The source code was reportedly uploaded to a file sharing site and then the link was posted to a malware forum.[28] This could be potentially dangerous if it gets into the hands of people who really know how to use it. The source code is written in C++ and requires someone with fairly good knowledge of C++ to figure out the code. [29] There are plenty of C++ hackers, however, who would

---

[24] "Cyber Banking Fraud: Global Partnerships Lead to Major Arrests." FBI. January 10, 2010. *www.fbi.gov/news/stories/2010/october/cyber-banking-fraud/cyber-banking-fraud* (accessed May 20, 2011).

[25] *Ibid.*

[26] *Ibid.*

[27] *Ibid.*

[28] Stevens, Kevin. "ZeuS Source Code Already in the Wild." TrendLabs Malware Blog. March 31, 2011. *http://blog.trendmicro.com/zeus-source-code-already-in-the-wild/* (accessed May 23, 2011).

[29] *Ibid.*

be able figure out this code and "improve" it for malicious purposes.

Not unlike a legitimate merger and acquisition, it has been confirmed as of March of 2011 that the creator of Zeus sold this source code to the people who make "SpyEye", another malware that is used to steal financial information.[30]

"SpyEye"

In December of 2009 a new malware toolkit known as "SpyEye" started to appear for sale on Russian underground forums. The starting price of this toolkit was $500.[31] Shortly afterwards, SpyEye became a competitor to Zeus and a contender for the "king of the banking bots" position. SpyEye and Zeus took their rivalry seriously, and the last version of SpyEye contained the feature "Kill Zeus."[32] The "Kill Zeus" feature actually removed Zeus from an infected system so only SpyEye would run.[33]

The creators of the SpyEye malware kit went out of their way to make it appealing and user-friendly with a user interface that rivals commercial applications. The main interface has a "Hack the Planet!" logo, and it displays how many bots are online and how many bots are currently part of the botnet.[34]

According to major antivirus software organizations, the merged SpyEye/Zeus bot toolkit has already been released into the hands of hackers who use it to create Trojan horses that infiltrate mobile devices.[35]

---

[30] *Ibid.*

[31] Coogan, Peter. "SpyEye Bot versus Zeus Bot." Symantec. February 22, 2010. *www.symantec.com/connect/blogs/spyeye-bot-versus-zeus-bot* (accessed May 13, 2011).

[32] *Ibid.*

[33] *Ibid.*

[34] Stevens, Kevin. "The SpyEye Interface, Part 1: CN 1." TrendLabs Malware Blog. October 3, 2010. *http://blog.trendmicro.com/the-spyeye-interface-part-1-cn-1/* (accessed May 23, 2011).

[35] Kharouni, Loucif. "SpyEye/ZeuS Toolkit v1.3.05 Beta." TrendLabs Malware Blog. January 24, 2011.

"Darkness" DDoS botnet tool

Another commercially available threat, which came to the attention of the cybersecurity community in 2010, is known as the "Darkness" botnet. It has rapidly proliferated in 2011, and still continues to gain momentum. Unlike Zeus and SpyEye, Darkness does not steal or spy. It spreads to create a DDoS network that is controlled by several domains hosted in Russia.[36] It goes after targets primarily in Europe and the USA.[37] Darkness is an example of malware as a service (MaaS).

The makers of this crimeware do not engage in attacks themselves, but rent their product out to others, and charge per number of sites and the amount of damage desired:

- 30 bots overwhelm an average site;
- 300 bots – a medium-sized site;
- 1,000 bots – a large site;
- 5,000 – a cluster of sites, even when using anti-DDoS blocks and other preventive measures.

Fifteen to twenty thousand bots can theoretically bring down a major social networking site.[38]

An attack on a large 1,000-bots' worth site sold for $50 a day.[39]

---

http://blog.trendmicro.com/spyeyezeus-toolkit-v1-3-05-beta/ (accessed May 24, 2011).

[36] Jackson Higgins, Kelly. "Active 'Darkness' DDoS Botnet's Tool Now Available For Free." *Dark Reading*. January 24, 2011. *www.darkreading.com/insiderthreat/167801100/security/attacks-breaches/229100144/active-darkness-ddos-botnet-s-tool-now-available-for-free.html* (accessed September 1, 2011).

[37] DiMino, Andre' M. "BlackEnergy competitor – The 'Darkness' DDoS Bot." Jeff Liford (dot) com. December 6, 2010. *http://jliford.blogspot.com/2010/12/blackenergy-competitor-darkness-ddos.html* (accessed August 1, 2011).

[38] Storm, Darlene. "Evil new DDoS botnet lurking in the Darkness." Computerworld. December 7, 2010. *http://blogs.computerworld.com/17489/evil_new_ddos_botnet_lurking_in_the_darkness*(accessed August 1, 2011).

[39] *Ibid.*

A higher-end version of Darkness that includes three different C&C servers, providing some built-in redundancy, costs about $350. This DDoS kit comes complete with the administration panel to create, dispatch, monitor, and control the army of bots that infects PCs all over the world.

In December of 2010, an older version of the Darkness code became available for free in various underground forums. The free release was followed by a slew of new Darkness botnet C&C servers waging DDoS attacks.[40]

---

[40] Jackson Higgins, Kelly. "Active 'Darkness' DDoS Botnet's Tool Now Available For Free." *Dark Reading*. January 24, 2011. *www.darkreading.com/insiderthreat/167801100/security/attacks-breaches/229100144/active-darkness-ddos-botnet-s-tool-now-available-for-free.html* (accessed September 1, 2011).

CHAPTER 3: UNINTENTIONAL CRIMEWARE

This chapter describes the "gray area" software: legitimate commercial software that is made for legitimate, non-criminal purposes, but which can be used by a malicious user to steal, disrupt, and manipulate.

SkyGrabber

The creators of SkyGrabber, a small Russian software company named SkySoftware, describe SkyGrabber as:

> offline satellite internet downloader. It accepts free to air (FTA) satellite data (movie, music, pictures) by digital satellite TV tuner card (DVB-S/DVB-S2) and saves information onto a hard disk. So, you'll get new movie, best music and funny pictures for free.
>
> You don't have to keep an online internet connection.[41]

It sounds innocent enough, although at second look this software could be entering a "gray area" of copyright infringement.

This $26 software was used by Iraqi insurgents in 2009 to hack into live video feeds from US Predator drones, providing the insurgents with information they needed to evade or monitor US military operations.[42] Granted, the US Air Force did not encrypt the video links, so it was an easy "hack" using regular COTS software and a little bit of ingenuity.

---

[41] "SkyGrabber". SkySoftware. *www.skygrabber.com/en/skygrabber.php* (accessed May 24, 2011).

[42] McCullagh, Declan. "Predator drones hacked in Iraq operations." CNET News. December 17, 2009. *http://news.cnet.com/8301-1009_3-10417247-83.html* (accessed April 7, 2011).

Passware Kit

The Mountain View, California company Passware.[43] released Passware Kit 10 in May of 2010. Passware Kit 10 is the first commercially available software to accelerate distributed password recovery using both software and hardware. At $795, Passware Kit 10 can utilize the computing power of multiple computers running Passware Kit Agents to increase performance in the password recovery process.[44]

Undoubtedly, recovering a strong password became much easier with the release of Passware Kit 10, due to its ability to connect multiple computers to one password recovery process.[45]

The IRS, US Army, US Department of Defense, US Department of Justice, US Department of Homeland Security, US Department of Transportation, US Postal Service, US Secret Service, US Senate, and US Supreme Court all are interested in becoming customers.[46] So are hackers and cybercriminals.

Maltego

Maltego by Paterva[47] represents data mining and data visualization software at its best. It seamlessly creates visual networks of interrelated data based on freely available open-source information. It reduces every piece of information into its basic components, such as "individual," "place," or "address." Every "entity" can be linked to other entities – people can be linked to addresses, for example. All different entities can be matched or grouped according to rules.[48] It can

---

[43] Passware. *www.lostpassword.com/.*

[44] "New Tool Speeds Password Cracking With Distributed Password Recovery." SecurityWeek News. May 25, 2010. *www.securityweek.com/new-tool-speeds-password-cracking-distributed-password-recovery* (accessed May 25, 2011).

[45] *Ibid.*

[46] *Ibid.*

[47] Maltego, *www.paterva.com/web5/* (accessed May 10, 2011).

[48] *Ibid.*

be applied to information from social networks to discover who is related to whom, personal e-mail addresses, phone numbers, and websites.

Law enforcement and intelligence communities are interested in Maltego. Large corporations want to visualize some of the internal data that they have.[49] Intelligence communities have used information visualization tools similar to Maltego to "connect the dots" and outline social networks among people, places, and events of interest for years. These tools, however, were either custom designed for a specific agency, or inaccessible to the mainstream users due to the cost. Now, Maltego is released as a "Community Edition," i.e. a free scaled-down version available to anyone.

Anyone who has a Facebook or LinkedIn page posts some information there. By itself this information can be relatively useless to someone who wishes to cause mischief. Linking this information, however, with other bits of publicly available information about a person throughout cyberspace can disclose enough to have his/her identity stolen or private information misused.

---

[49] Buley, Taylor. "When Everyone Can Mine Your Data." Forbes.com LLC™. November 21, 2008. *www.forbes.com/2008/11/21/maltego-data-mining-identity08-tech-cz-tb_1121maltego.html* (accessed May 23, 2011).

CHAPTER 4: THE PRESENT AND THE FUTURE

"Kill with a borrowed knife" is one of 36 Chinese Stratagems.[50] Is commercially available malware such a knife? Granted, governments cannot really control what hackers are doing and their entrepreneurial drivers, but can that be influenced?

Governments, being aware of the strengths and weaknesses of their adversaries, are hurriedly forging cyberwarfare conventions and agreements.[51] Although everyone is aware of the threat, nobody wants to be engaged in full-blown cyberwarfare with a technically savvy adversary. Besides, engaging in cyberwarfare on a state level may constitute a declaration of war, and conventional warfare, especially among the super-powers, is highly undesirable to all.[52]

There is a way, however, to maintain deniability and yet engage in a cyber conflict, through the deeds of "rogue hackers." This could be done through indirect influences, such as propaganda, relaxed or non-existent laws regarding creating and distributing malware, and making tools of hacking directly available to the less technically savvy masses when the time is right.

The phenomenon of hacktivism – described earlier in this pocket guide – could be manipulated and turned against the

---

[50] Carr, Jeffrey. *Inside Cyber Warfare: Mapping the Cyber Underworld.* O'Reilly Media, 2009. p.174.

[51] Rauscher, Karl Frederick, and Andrey Korotkov. "Russia-U.S. Bilateral on Critical Infrastructure Protection: Working Towards Rules for Governing Cyber Conflict: Rendering the Geneva and Hague Conventions in Cyberspace." "An advance publication of this paper was presented at the Munich Security Conference, February 4-6, 2011." New York, NY: The EastWest Institute, 2011.

[52] Schneier, Bruce. "Cyberwar." Schneier on Security. June 4, 2007. *www.schneier.com/blog/archives/2007/06/cyberwar.html* (accessed May 20, 2011), and Lt. Com Matthew Skeletov via Carr, Jeffrey. *Inside Cyber Warfare: Mapping the Cyber Underworld.* O'Reilly Media, 2009. p.47.

state adversary while the government can deny an act of cyberwar.[53] The scale and magnitude of cyberattacks on Estonia and Georgia using DDoS attacks suggests that many individuals were involved in the attacks, and it also suggests that somehow the tools of these attacks were readily available to them. In this case, the malware attacks were conducted in one cyber carpet bombing effort, and the hacktivist leaders claimed responsibility while the Russian government actively denied participation.[54]

The same situation is currently happening between China and the US, but in a slow, deliberate motion. Since 2003, an extensive cyber-penetration effort by Chinese hackers, called Titan Rain, has continuously been targeting US research, military, and commercial networks.[55] There is a large variety of commercial and free malware toolkits available for wannabe hackers in China, who are backed by Maoist ideology and no repercussions for infiltrating American military and civil infrastructures … as the Chinese government denies the involvement.[56]

To be fair, the United States, UK, and Australia probably have a similar strategy in place, including manipulation of hacktivist culture and making malware easily accessible when the time is right. In fact, the military of the US is actually looking into the "botnet" paradigm as a deterrent and an attack mechanism in the case of a cyber conflict.[57]

---

[53] Krapp, Peter. "Terror and Play, or What Was Hacktivism?" *Grey Room* no. 21 (Fall 2005): 70–93. *Academic Search™ Premier*, EBSCO*host*® (accessed May 14, 2011).

[54] Carr, Jeffrey. *Inside Cyber Warfare: Mapping the Cyber Underworld*. O'Reilly Media, 2009. pp.3, 15, 18, 37.

[55] Stiennon, Richard. *Surviving Cyberwar*. Lanham, MD: Government Institutes, 2010. p.42.

[56] Hagestad II, William. "China: A Comparative Analysis of Government & Nationalistic Threat Vectors." Central Ohio InfoSec Summit, Columbus, OH. 2011.

[57] Williamson III, Charles W. "Carpet bombing in cyberspace: Why America needs a military botnet." *Armed Forces Journal*. *www.armedforcesjournal.com/2008/05/3375884* (accessed May 26, 2011).

And, of course, internal political motivation can be reason for cyber-attacks. Hacker groups Anonymous and LulzSec have launched attacks targeted at NASA, the CIA and Sony Pictures to steal confidential data and disrupt operations.[58] In February of 2010 Australian government websites were brought down by the Anonymous online community using DDoS attacks. These attacks were launched in response to proposed web censorship regulations.[59]

These widespread attacks could be accomplished only with the use of commercially available or free malware toolkits.

---

[58] Sapre, Omkar. "Cyber underworld: How it works." The Times of India. September 22, 2011. *http://timesofindia.indiatimes.com/tech/enterprise-it/security/Cyber-underworld-How-it-works/articleshow/10075465.cms* (accessed September 23, 2011).

[59] *Ibid.*

CHAPTER 5: FIGHTING BACK

Criminal use of malware is in the middle of an evolutionary curve. Their capabilities, target platforms and creative uses are about to enter a period of rapid change and deeper, enhanced infection vectors. Organizations without the capability to identify anomalies in their environment via monitoring tools and honeypot technologies will simply become the most compromised victims in the long term.

L. Brent Huston, @lbhuston, CEO and Security Evangelist, MicroSolved, Inc.

How to protect yourself from botnet infections

Secure software and smart security practices, such as the ones listed below, are the keys to protecting yourself and your system from cyber theft and from becoming a zombie computer in a bot network.

- Antivirus and anti-spyware software is essential to every system. It is important to keep it regularly updated. A comprehensive list of major antivirus software packages is found at *http://en.wikipedia.org/wiki/List_of_antivirus_software.*
- Keep the operating system patched against known vulnerabilities by enabling automated patches.
- Keep software installed in your system patched against the known vulnerabilities. Security patches are usually free and can be downloaded from the software vendors.
- Use a correctly configured personal firewall to protect your computer from unauthorized access.
- Be careful on the World Wide Web. Use common-sense web surfing practices and anti-malicious website protection provided by major antivirus producers.
- Disconnect your computer from the Internet, when you are not using it.

- Exercise caution when opening attachments or following links in e-mails and on websites.
- Research before downloading new, unknown software.
- Never reveal your passwords over the phone or via e-mail.
- Exercise good judgment when posting personal information on social websites and forums.

Active defense

As malware tools continue to evolve, so do the defense systems against them. Firewall, antivirus, and anti-malware software applications hold a prominent place in every personal and organizational computer system or network. And yet it has been acknowledged by the cybersecurity industry that these defense systems only catch about 25% of all malware attacks.[60]

A passive defense aimed at preventing compromise by malicious code is not enough. Active defense techniques are beginning to evolve, such as confusing and frustrating the attacker, as well as counterattacking by exploiting the attacker's vulnerabilities.

Research on counterattacking, also known as aggressive self-defense, active defense, or strike-back, has taken place for many years. The counterattacks range from passive approaches to full remote exploitation, and popular tools to gain information about attackers include honeypots and honeynets.[61] Honeypots and honeynets are traps set to detect, deflect, or corrupt malware attacks on individual computers or networks.[62]

Many antivirus firms and other research organizations have run large honeynets to collect malware and attack signatures.[63]

---

[60] Ollmann, Gunter. "How Criminals Build Botnets for Profit." Central Ohio InfoSec Summit, Columbus, OH. 2011.

[61] Weeks, Matthew. "Counterattack: Turning the tables on exploitation attempts from tools like Metasploit." Black Hat™, Crystal City. 2011

[62] *Ibid.*

[63] *Ibid.*

These organizations research and implement counterattacks to deceive, crash, exploit, or just get information on attackers.

One such organization, MicroSolved, Inc. (*www.microsolved.com*), provides a product, HoneyPoint, which fools attackers into believing that they are attacking defenseless applications, while in reality they are triggering sensors that are catching them "in the act." By doing the things attackers do, such as scanning ports, connecting to services, and probing for vulnerabilities, they are giving away their presence and tactics.[64]

There has even been a suggestion to use software agents to scout networks and seek and destroy botnets.[65] Agents are defined as programs that autonomously acquire, manipulate, distribute, and maintain information on behalf of cybersecurity forces.[66]

Although there is some legal controversy regarding the use of active defenses, it is the most effective deterrent to date. Once the commercially sold botnets become easily detectable and ineffective, the market value of these botnets will decrease, and so will the desire by third parties to buy and use them.

[64] MicroSolved, Inc., *www.microsolved.com*.
[65] Dembskey, Evan, and Elmarie Biermann. "Towards an Intelligent Software Agent System as Defense against Botnets." Proceedings of the 6th International Conference on Information Warfare and Security, The George Washington University, Washington, DC, USA, 17–18 March 2011. Reading, UK: Academic Publishing International Limited, 2011. 299–307.
[66] *Ibid.*

CONCLUSION

Commercialization of malware evolved into its own underground economy, complete with competing organizations, well-defined business models, and mergers and acquisitions. The phenomenon of having malware construction kits available to anyone creates a continuously morphing geographically and politically distributed attack vehicle that is difficult to detect and defend against.[67] More people with "criminal intent," who previously did not have the tools and the know-how to steal and defraud online, now have this ability along with the tools. What is worse, since the ability of releasing malware into cyberspace is accessible to the masses, these masses can be manipulated or persuaded by governments to launch cyberattacks against their adversaries without "officially" engaging in acts of cyberwarfare.

It has been mandated by the US President Barack Obama to:

> … continue to invest in the cutting-edge research and development necessary for the innovation and discovery we need to meet the digital challenges of our time.[68]

Innovative actions against commercially available malware will be at least a part of the solution.

Reactive defenses, such as firewalls and antivirus checks, are no longer effective. The only way to deter the "entrepreneurs" of the malware underworld and their consumers is to turn their weapons against them. It means actively striking back using specialized botnets, viruses, and software agents directed at the makers and the consumers of such malware, striking them at the source, exposing their identities, and disabling their own computers and networks.

---

[67] Ollmann, Gunter. "How Criminals Build Botnets for Profit." Central Ohio InfoSec Summit, Columbus, OH. 2011.

[68] Obama, Barack. "Remarks By The President On Securing Our Nation's Cyber Infrastructure." The White House. May 29, 2009. *www.whitehouse.gov/the-press-office/remarks-president-securing-our-nations-cyber-infrastructure* (accessed April 30, 2011).

Conclusion

While there are various laws and statutes to deal with those who employ computer programs such as viruses or even "unintended malware" to:

> infect other computer programs or computer data, consume resources, modify, destroy, record or transmit data, and disrupt normal operation of a computer system,[69]

there are, it would appear, no adequate laws to deal with producers of malware toolkits.[70] Special laws should be established to criminalize production of malware components for sale as well as for buying them, even if the producers or buyers themselves do not use them.

Will these measures completely deter all the producers and consumers of malware toolkits? These measures will probably not deter all, but they will deter some – and this is a start.

---

[69] Virus/Contaminant/Destructive Transmission Statutes, National Conference of State Legislatures. *www.ncsl.org/default.aspx?tabid=13487* (accessed May 28, 2011).

[70] Ollmann, Gunter. "How Criminals Build Botnets for Profit." Central Ohio InfoSec Summit, Columbus, OH. 2011.

AUTHORITATIVE SOURCES OF INFORMATION

Malware evolves and morphs at neck-breaking speed, and it is almost impossible to keep up with new developments. Therefore, any book or article in a scholarly journal on malware and its commercialization will become obsolete by the time it is released off the press.

Having said that, *Hacking: The Next Generation* by Nitesh Dhanjani, Billy Rios, and Brett Hardin[71] provides software code examples and a good technical background on the most common types of malware, attack vectors, and defense mechanisms. In addition, the book by Jeffrey Carr, *Inside Cyber Warfare: Mapping the Cyber Underworld,*[72] is probably the most comprehensive information available on understanding cyberwarfare and its actors.

The most authoritative, up-to-date sources on the topic of commercial malware are the same people and organizations that make their living fighting it. Blogs and articles from cybersecurity and antivirus organizations like Symantec (*www.symantec.com*), McAfee (*http://blogs.mcafee.com/*), Kaspersky (*www.kaspersky.com/*), and TrendMicro (*http://blog.trendmicro.com/*) provide the most up-to-date information on commercially available malware, how it functions, how it is distributed, and how to fight it.

Interesting and new knowledge is shared at special conferences, such as InfoSec,[73] DerbyCon,[74] DEF CON,[75] and Black Hat™.[76] Although DEF CON and Black Hat™ are dubbed as "hacker" conferences, these conferences are actually

[71] Dhanjani, Nitesh, Billy Rios, Brett Hardin. *Hacking: The Next Generation*. O'Reilly Media, 2009.
[72] Carr, Jeffrey. *Inside Cyber Warfare: Mapping the Cyber Underworld*. O'Reilly Media, 2009.
[73] Central Ohio InfoSec Summit. *www.infosecsummit.com/*.
[74] DerbyCon conference. *www.derbycon.com/*.
[75] DEF CON conference. *www.defcon.org/*.
[76] Black Hat™ conference. *www.blackhat.com/*.

about researching and explaining how malware works, how it is distributed and used, and how it can be fought.

The speakers at these conferences are usually the sources of the new information and knowledge. One of the utmost experts and prolific authors on everything concerning malware – its design, development, and commercialization – is Gunter Ollmann, VP of Research of Damballa.[77] He presents at cybersecurity-related conferences and publishes a blog and numerous white papers on his corporate website.

Finally, an internationally renowned security technologist and author, Bruce Schneier,[78] provides very comprehensive and candid cybersecurity information and commentary.

---

[77] Damballa. *www.damballa.com*, and *http://technicalinfodotnet.blogspot.com/* (accessed May 21, 2011).
[78] Schneier, Bruce. Schneier on Security. *www.schneier.com/blog/archives/2007/06/cyberwar.html*.

BIBLIOGRAPHY

Baker, Wade, Alexander Hutton, C. David Hylender, et. al. "2011 Data Breach Investigations Report: A study conducted by the Verizon RISK Team with cooperation from the U.S. Secret Service and the Dutch High Tech Crime Unit." Verizon, 2011.

Black Hat™ conference. *www.blackhat.com/*.

"bot worm". SearchSecurity. *http://searchsecurity.techtarget.com/definition/bot-worm* (accessed 30 November 2011).

Brown, Francis, and Rob Ragan. "Lord of the Bing: Taking Back Search Engine Hacking From Google and Bing." Presentation at Black Hat™ USA 2010. Stach & Liu, LLC, 2010.

Buley, Taylor. "When Everyone Can Mine Your Data." Forbes.com LLC™. November 21, 2008. *www.forbes.com/2008/11/21/maltego-data-mining-identity08-tech-cz-tb_1121maltego.html* (accessed May 23, 2011).

Carr, Jeffrey. *Inside Cyber Warfare: Mapping the Cyber Underworld.* O'Reilly Media, 2009.

Central Ohio InfoSec Summit. *www.infosecsummit.com/*.

Chapman, Glenn. "Internet warriors hone skills at Black Hat – DefCon." Yahoo! Singapore Finance News. July 26, 2010. *http://sg.finance.yahoo.com/news/Internet-warriors-hone-skills-afpsg-2628024338.html?x=0* (accessed May 2, 2011).

Coleman, Kevin. "Cyber Intelligence – the Key to All Cyber Operations." Defense Tech. November 15, 2010. *http://defensetech.org/2010/11/15/cyber-intelligence-%e2%80%93-the-key-to-all-cyber-operations/* (accessed May 13, 2011).

Coogan, Peter. "SpyEye Bot versus Zeus Bot." Symantec. February 22, 2010. *www.symantec.com/connect/blogs/spyeye-bot-versus-zeus-bot* (accessed May 13, 2011).

"Cyber Banking Fraud: Global Partnerships Lead to Major Arrests." FBI. January 10, 2010. *www.fbi.gov/news/stories/2010/october/cyber-banking-fraud/cyber-banking-fraud* (accessed May 20, 2011).

Damballa. *www.damballa.com* (accessed May 21, 2011).

Danchev, Dancho. "New report details the prices within the cybercrime market." ZDNet. February 7, 2011. *www.zdnet.com/blog/security/new-report-details-the-prices-within-the-cybercrime-market/8078?tag=nl.e550* (accessed May 13, 2011).

DEF CON conference. *www.defcon.org/*.

Dembskey, Evan, and Elmarie Biermann. "Towards an Intelligent Software Agent System as Defense against Botnets." Proceedings of the 6th International Conference on Information Warfare and Security, The George Washington University, Washington, DC, USA, 17–18 March 2011. Reading, UK: Academic Publishing International Limited, 2011. 299-307.

DerbyCon conference. *www.derbycon.com/*.

Dhanjani, Nitesh, Billy Rios, Brett Hardin. *Hacking: The Next Generation.* O'Reilly Media, 2009.

DiMino, Andre' M. "BlackEnergy competitor – The 'Darkness' DDoS Bot." Jeff Liford (dot) com. December 6, 2010. *http://jliford.blogspot.com/2010/12/blackenergy-competitor-darkness-ddos.html* (accessed August 1, 2011).

Falliere, Nicolas, and Eric Chien. "Zeus: King of the Bots." Symantec Security Response. *www.symantec.com/content/en/us/enterprise/media/security_response/whitepapers/zeus_king_of_bots.pdf* (accessed May 23, 2011).

Fialka, John J. *War by Other Means: Economic Espionage in America*. New York: W.W. Norton and Company, 1999.

Gjelten, Tom. "Cyberwarrior Shortage Threatens U.S. Security." NPR. July 19, 2010. *www.npr.org/templates/story/story.php?storyId=128574055* (accessed May 13, 2011).

Goodman, Will. "Cyber Deterrence: Tougher in Theory than in Practice?" *Strategic Studies Quarterly*, Fall 2010: 102–135.

"hacktivism." SearchSecurity. *http://searchsecurity.techtarget.com/definition/hacktivism* (accessed May 27, 2011).

Hagestad II, William. "China: A Comparative Analysis of Government & Nationalistic Threat Vectors." Central Ohio InfoSec Summit, Columbus, OH. 2011.

Harris, Shane. "China's Cyber-Militia." *National Journal*. May 31, 2008. *http://nationaljournal.com/magazine/china-s-cyber-militia-20080531* (accessed April 20, 2011).

Howard, Fraser. "Night Dragon attacks: myth or reality?" Naked Security. February 11, 2011. *http://nakedsecurity.sophos.com/2011/02/11/night-dragon-attacks-myth-or-reality/* (accessed April 22, 2011).

HPCR Manual on International Law Applicable to Air and Missile Warfare. Program on Humanitarian Policy and Conflict Research, Harvard University. 2010. *www.ihlresearch.org/amw/manual/section-a-definitions/m* (accessed May 27, 2011).

http://technicalinfodotnet.blogspot.com/ (accessed May 21, 2011).

Jackson Higgins, Kelly. "Active 'Darkness' DDoS Botnet's Tool Now Available For Free." *Dark Reading*. January 24, 2011. *www.darkreading.com/insiderthreat/167801100/security/attacks-breaches/229100144/active-darkness-ddos-botnet-s-tool-now-available-for-free.html* (accessed September 1, 2011).

Kharouni, Loucif. "SpyEye/ZeuS Toolkit v1.3.05 Beta." TrendLabs Malware Blog. January 24, 2011. *http://blog.trendmicro.com/spyeyezeus-toolkit-v1-3-05-beta/* (accessed May 24, 2011).

Krapp, Peter. "Terror and Play, or What Was Hacktivism?" *Grey Room* no. 21 (Fall 2005): 70-93. *Academic Search™ Premier*, EBSCO*host*® (accessed May 14, 2011).

"Malware becoming increasingly commercialised, says CoreTrace." *InfoSecurity*. February 2, 2011. *www.infosecurity-magazine.com/view/15623/malware-becoming-increasingly-commercialised-says-coretrace/* (accessed May 10, 2011).

McAfee. "How to Protect Your Computer Against Virus and Worm Attacks." McAfee Security Advice Center. 2011. *http://home.mcafee.com/AdviceCenter/Default.aspx?id=ad_vp_htpycavawa* (accessed March 30, 2011). (Please note: this reference may not be accessible via this web address from some locations.)

McAfee® Foundstone® Professional Services and McAfee Labs™. "Global Energy Cyberattacks: "Night Dragon"." McAfee. February 10, 2011. *www.mcafee.com/us/resources/white-papers/wp-global-energy-cyberattacks-night-dragon.pdf* (accessed April 23, 2011).

McCullagh, Declan. "Predator drones hacked in Iraq operations." CNET News. December 17, 2009. *http://news.cnet.com/8301-1009_3-10417247-83.html* (accessed April 7, 2011).

Mehan, Julie E. *Cyberwar, Cyberterror, Cybercrime: A Guide to the Role of Standards in an Environment of Change and Danger*. UK: IT Governance Publishing, 2008.

"Microsoft Security Bulletin MS08-067 – Critical". Microsoft TechNet. October 23, 2008. *www.microsoft.com/technet/security/bulletin/ms08-067.mspx* (accessed May 23, 2011).

"Military Command Uses Bit9 Parity to Thwart 'Red Team' Attack." White paper, Case Study United States Military Command. Waltham, MA: Bit9. 2009.

Mitnick, Kevin D., and William L. Simon. *The Art Of Intrusion: The Real Stories Behind the Exploits of Hackers, Intruders and Deceivers*. Indianapolis, IN: Wiley Publishing, Inc. 2005.

Nagaraja, Shishir, and Ross Anderson. "The snooping dragon: social-malware surveillance of the Tibetan movement." Technical Report Number 746. Cambridge, UK: University of Cambridge Computer Laboratory, 2009.

"New Tool Speeds Password Cracking With Distributed Password Recovery." SecurityWeek News. May 25, 2010. *www.securityweek.com/new-tool-speeds-password-cracking-distributed-password-recovery* (accessed May 25, 2011).

Obama, Barack. "Remarks By The President On Securing Our Nation's Cyber Infrastructure." The White House. May 29, 2009. *www.whitehouse.gov/the-press-office/remarks-president-securing-our-nations-cyber-infrastructure* (accessed April 30, 2011).

Ollmann, Gunter. "How Criminals Build Botnets for Profit." Central Ohio InfoSec Summit, Columbus, OH. 2011.

Percoco, Nicholas J., and Jibran Ilyas. "Malware Freakshow 2010". A white paper for Black Hat™ USA 2010. Trustwave, 2010.

Pincus, Walter. "Government devotes more brainpower and money to cybersecurity." *The Washington Post*. June 22, 2010. *www.washingtonpost.com/wp-dyn/content/article/2010/06/21/AR2010062104680.html* (accessed August 12, 2010).

Rauscher, Karl Frederick, and Andrey Korotkov. "Russia-U.S. Bilateral on Critical Infrastructure Protection: Working Towards Rules for Governing Cyber Conflict: Rendering the Geneva and Hague Conventions in Cyberspace." "An advance publication of this paper was presented at the Munich Security

Conference, February 4-6, 2011." New York, NY: The EastWest Institute, 2011.

Ren, Haowei. "Exploit-MS08-067 Bundled in Commercial Malware Kit." McAfee Labs. November 14, 2008. *http://blogs.mcafee.com/mcafee-labs/exploit-ms08-067-bundled-in-commercial-malware-kit* (accessed May 23, 2011).

"Report on Attack Toolkits and Malicious Websites." Symantec. *www.symantec.com/about/news/resources/press_kits/detail.jsp?pkid=attackkits&om_ext_cid=biz_socmed_twitter_facebook_marketwire_linkedin_2011Jan_worldwide_attacktoolkits* (accessed May 27, 2011).

Robinson, Colin. "Military and Cyber-Defense: Reactions to the Threat." CDI Terrorism Project. November 8, 2002. *http://www.cdi.org/terrorism/cyberdefense-pr.cfm*(accessed April 16, 2011).

Rohret, David, and Jonathan Holston. "Exploitation of Blue Team SATCOM and MILSAT Assets for Red Team Covert Exploitation and Back-Channel Communications." *Proceedings of the International Conference on Information Warfare & Security*. 2010. 288-298. *International Security & Counter-Terrorism Reference Center*™, EBSCO*host*® (accessed May 14, 2011).

Sapre, Omkar. "Cyber underworld: How it works." The Times of India. September 22, 2011. *http://timesofindia.indiatimes.com/tech/enterprise-it/security/Cyber-underworld-How-it-works/articleshow/10075465.cms* (accessed September 23, 2011).

Schmidt, Howard A. "Transparent Cybersecurity." The White House. March 2, 2010. *www.whitehouse.gov/blog/2010/03/02/transparent-cybersecurity* (accessed May 2, 2011).

Schneier, Bruce. "Cyberwar." Schneier on Security. June 4, 2007. *www.schneier.com/blog/archives/2007/06/cyberwar.html* (accessed May 20, 2011).

"Scottish University Opening School For Hackers." Edudemic. May 13, 2011. *http://edudemic.com/2011/05/scottish-university-opening-school-for-hackers/* (accessed May 14, 2011).

Sommer, Peter, and Ian Brown. "Reducing Systemic Cybersecurity Risk." OECD/IFP Project on "Future Global Shocks". OECD, 2011.

Stevens, Kevin. "The SpyEye Interface, Part 1: CN 1." TrendLabs Malware Blog. October 3, 2010. *http://blog.trendmicro.com/the-spyeye-interface-part-1-cn-1/* (accessed May 23, 2011).

Stevens, Kevin. "ZeuS Source Code Already in the Wild." TrendLabs Malware Blog. March 31, 2011. *http://blog.trendmicro.com/zeus-source-code-already-in-the-wild/* (accessed May 23, 2011).

Stevens, Kevin, and Don Jackson. "ZeuS Banking Trojan Report." Dell SecureWorks. March 11, 2010. *www.secureworks.com/research/threats/zeus/?threat=zeus* (accessed May 19, 2010).

Stiennon, Richard. *Surviving Cyberwar*. Lanham, MD: Government Institutes, 2010.

Storm, Darlene. "Evil new DDoS botnet lurking in the Darkness." Computerworld. December 7, 2010. *http://blogs.computerworld.com/17489/evil_new_ddos_botnet_lurking_in_the_darkness* (accessed August 1, 2011).

Virus/Contaminant/Destructive Transmission Statutes, National Conference of State Legislatures. *www.ncsl.org/default.aspx?tabid=13487* (accessed May 28, 2011).

Weeks, Matthew. "Counterattack: Turning the tables on exploitation attempts from tools like Metasploit." Black Hat™, Crystal City. 2011.

Williamson III, Charles W. "Carpet bombing in cyberspace: Why America needs a military botnet." *Armed Forces Journal*.

www.armedforcesjournal.com/2008/05/3375884 (accessed May 26, 2011).

EU for product safety is Stephen Evans, The Mill Enterprise Hub, Stagreenan, Drogheda, Co. Louth, A92 CD3D, Ireland. (servicecentre@itgovernance.eu)

www.ingramcontent.com/pod-product-compliance
Lightning Source LLC
LaVergne TN
LVHW012335100826
845148LV00017B/2636

* 9 7 8 1 8 4 9 2 8 3 2 8 1 *